Contents

These children are all **Muslims**. There are Muslims all over the world.

My Muslim Life

Riadh El-Droubie

WAYLAND

LOOKING AT RELIGION

My Buddhist Life
My Christian Life
My Hindu Life
My Jewish Life
My Muslim Life
My Sikh Life

Editor: Ruth Raudsepp
Designer: Joyce Chester

First published in Great Britain in 1996 by Wayland (Publishers) Ltd under the series title 'Everyday Religion'
This edition published in 2006 by Hodder Wayland, an imprint of Hodder Children's Books

Reprinted in 2007 by Wayland, an imprint of Hachette Children's Books

Hachette Children's Books, 338 Euston Road, London NW1 3BH

A catalogue record for this book is available from the British Library

ISBN-13: 978 0 7502 4956 0

Picture acknowledgements
The publishers would like to thank the following for allowing their photographs to be used in this book: Circa Photo Library title page, Eye Ubiquitous 11, 16; Rupert Horrox cover; Hutchison 4 (top right), 7, 24; Peter Sanders 4 (top left and bottom), 5, 6, 8, 9, 10, 12, 13, 14, 15, 17, 18, 19, 20, 21, 22, 23, 25, 26. Artwork on page 27 is supplied by Riadh El-Droubie.

Title page: Muslim girls studying at school.

Typeset by Joyce Chester
Printed in China

Nabil is a newborn baby.
The first words he hears are
the call to prayer.

Muslim children learn to read the
Qur'an when they are very young.
Jameel is learning to read the
Qur'an with his father.

On Sundays Mustafa and Ahmad
go to the **mosque** school to learn
about **Islam**.

Muslims pray five times a day to show their thanks to **Allah**. This prayer is called 'Salat'.

Muslims must wash themselves
before prayer.

Yasmin is praying to God. She does not always go to the mosque to pray, she can pray anywhere.

Friday is a very special day for Muslims. They go to the mosque at midday to pray and meet friends.

Muslims face towards the **Ka'bah** at **Makkah** when they pray. Makkah is a very important place for Muslims.

One wall inside the mosque shows
the direction of Makkah.

Hasan and his sister Layla use a special compass to find the direction of Makkah.

Muslims try to visit Makkah at least
once in their lives. This special
journey is called **Hajj**.

Muslims celebrate the festival of **Id-ul-Adha** after Hajj. The food is shared with friends and neighbours.

After Hajj Muslims travel to **Madinah** to visit the **Prophet**'s Mosque.

On their way home after Hajj Muslims travel to Jerusalem to visit the Al-Aqsa Mosque and the Dome of the Rock.

Following Hajj, the Muslim New Year begins. Muslims celebrate with stories about the Prophet's journey from Makkah to Madinah.

Kareem points to the new moon. With the new moon **Ramadan** begins. Muslims do not eat or drink between sunrise and sunset during the month of Ramadan.

When the sun has gone down
Muslims can stop **fasting**. They
begin their meal with dates and
water, and then they pray.

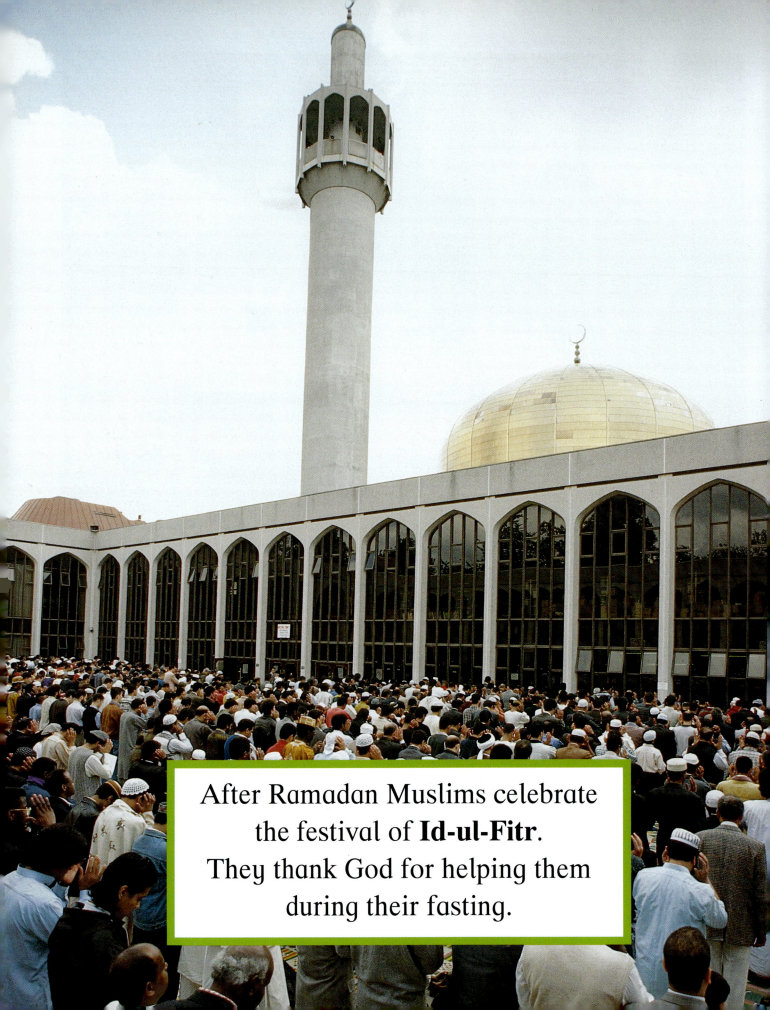

After Ramadan Muslims celebrate
the festival of **Id-ul-Fitr**.
They thank God for helping them
during their fasting.

On Id day Muslims think of others and give money when they visit the mosque.

Najwa and Halima dress in their best clothes for Id day celebrations.

Hind and her mother send Id cards
to friends wishing them happiness
on Id day.

Yusuf and Akram greet each other on Id day, they say 'Id Mubarak'.

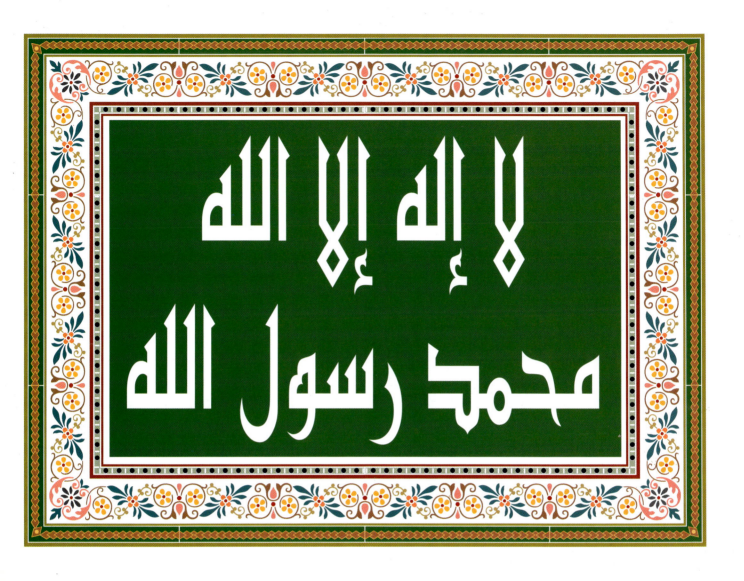

The first thing Muslims learn is
'There is only one God and
Muhammad ﷺ is His last
Messenger.'

Notes for Teachers

It is customary among Muslims to show their respect for the Prophet Muhammad by saying 'Peace and blessing of God be upon him' whenever the name is spoken. In print the symbol ﷺ is used to represent these words. Similarly the names of all the Prophets are followed by the words 'Peace be upon him' (pbuh).

Pages 4 and 5 The initiation ceremony is called 'Aqeeqah'. After recitation of some passages from the Qur'an, the call to prayer, the Adhan, is whispered in a newborn baby's ears:

Allah is most Great (four times)

I testify there is no god but Allah (twice)

I testify that Muhammad is the Messenger of Allah (twice)

Hasten to prayer (twice)

Hasten to prosperity (twice)

Allah is most Great (twice)

There is no god but Allah (once)

Then the name of the child is declared. A feast follows and charity is given to the needy.

Pages 6 and 7 The Qur'an is the first of two main sources of guidance. The life and tradition of Prophet Muhammad ﷺ is the second source. For Muslims the Qur'an is the word of God revealed to the Prophet in the Arabic language. It contains guidance in all aspects of life. As Islam considers life on earth as one unit, there is no division between sacred and worldly affairs. All actions of a Muslim must be for the sake of God.

Pages 8 and 9 The five daily prayers are called *Salat*. Following the teaching of the Qur'an and the tradition of the Prophet Muhammad ﷺ, Muslims must be clean in body and in heart. Before *Salat*, they wash their hands, mouth, nose, face, arms and feet in running water in order and manner followed by the Prophet ﷺ. This is called *Wudu.*

Pages 10 and 11 Friday is an important day for Muslims. It is a day of celebration and collective worship at the mosque. In Muslim countries government offices are closed on this day, but usual daily activities take place as normal before and after Friday prayer.

There is no priesthood in Islam. The Imam advises people and leads them in prayers. Every person may approach God at any time and at any place. Muslims can pray anywhere, at the mosque, office or at home. They can pray alone or in a group provided the place is clean. A prayer mat may be used.

Pages 12 and 13 The Ka'bah is the focus of Muslim worship and the first mosque on earth. The first act of Prophet Muhammad ﷺ, when he reached Madinah after his migration from Makkah, was to build a mosque where he taught his followers their faith. It became the central office for his government. Today, the mosque is the central place for a Muslim community's activities. At prayer in the mosque, everyone faces the niche, the *mirab*, which marks the direction of Makkah.

Pages 14 and 15 Makkah holds great significance as a spiritual centre for Muslims. The pilgrimage to Makkah (Hajj), the fourth pillar of Islam, is a journey every Muslim hopes to make. It is a duty for those who can afford the journey and who are physically well to make the pilgrimage at least once in his or her life time. Hundreds of thousands of pilgrims arrive in Makkah to visit the grand mosque in which stands the Ka'bah, a cube shaped building. The Qur'an tells that Abraham (peace be upon him) and his son, Isma'il (peace be upon him), built the Ka'bah as a place of worship in Makkah.

Pages 16 and 17 The festival of Id-ul-Adha commemorates the sacrifice Prophet Abraham (peace be upon him) was willing to make of his son Isma'il (peace be upon him). On the first day of Id-ul-Adha Muslims sacrifice a lamb and share the food in keeping with the tradition of Prophet Abraham (peace be upon him).

Muslims believe that prophet Mohammad ﷺ was the final prophet sent by God as a guide to all humankind. He had no authority to change the message he received from God, his duty was to deliver and explain the message of God and to be an example to humankind. The Qur'an commands Muslims to follow in his footsteps.

Pages 18 and 19 Jerusalem is important to Muslims because it is the place where the prophet Muhammad ﷺ went through on his ascension to the heavens. In heaven he received the command of the five daily prayers. It is believed that he met with all other prophets near Al-Aqsa Mosque close to the famous rock where the shrine, the Dome of the Rock, now stands.

Muslims throughout the world use a lunar calendar. A month is counted from one new moon to the next, lasting between 29 or 30 days. The Islamic year marks the time when Prophet Muhammad ﷺ migrated from Makkah to Madinah and established the first Islamic state. For Muslims, this event, the Hijrah, is a significant episode in the history of Islam.

Pages 20 and 21 Fasting is the fifth pillar of Islam, and takes place during Ramadan, the ninth month of the Muslim calendar. Every day, from dawn to dusk, Muslims do not eat or drink. During this month greater attention is paid to reading the Qur'an and to prayers. Fasting helps Muslims to identify with those people who are hungry and to be appreciative of all good things given to them by God. The sick, the very old and young, nursing mothers and travellers are excused from fasting, but they are expected to fast later

for any days missed. During Ramadan the day often begins very early as families eat before dawn. At sunset, the fast is broken with a drink of water and a few dates before a main meal is eaten after sunset prayer.

Pages 22 and 23 Ramadan is a time of sharing and togetherness. All Muslims, whether rich or poor, fast together and experience the same feelings of hunger and hardship. The end of Ramadan is marked by the festival of Id-ul-Fitr. At the sighting of the new moon there is great rejoicing and celebrating. Id-ul-Fitr means 'festival of breaking the fast' and lasts for three days. Families and friends celebrate together, Id cards are sent and everyone dresses in their best clothes. The first day of Id begins with early breakfast, followed by a visit to the mosque for Id prayer. Id greetings are exchanged by saying 'Id Mubarak', which means a happy and blessed Id. Id is also a time of sharing. Muslims give Zakah, an annual payment of welfare tax. This is an obligatory act of worship, and the zakah is used to help people in need.

Pages 24, 25 and 26 There are two Id festivals in Islam. The first day of each Id begins with prayers at the mosque. The rest of the day is spent in alms-giving and visiting friends and relatives to exchange greetings. The first Id festival is Id-ul-Fitr (the festival of breaking the fast). It lasts three days and is celebrated at the end of Ramadan. The second Id festival is Id-ul-Adha and is celebrated at the end of Hajj (pilgrimage to Makkah). It lasts for four days. On the first day following Id prayer, Muslims sacrifice a lamb or cow and share the meat with those less fortunate.

Page 27 Central to the Muslim faith is the declaration that 'There is no god but Allah and Muhammad ﷺ is the Messenger of Allah.' This declaration of faith, called the *Shahadah*, is the first of the five pillars of Islam (the religious duties upon which Islam rests).

Glossary

Allah The Arabic name for God.

fasting To stop eating and drinking for a period of time.

Hajj The special journey many Muslims make to Makkah once in their lives.

Id-ul-Adha A festival Muslims celebrate at the end of Hajj.

Id-ul-Fitr A festival held at the end of Ramadan.

Islam The religion and way of life that Muslims follow.

Ka'bah A cube-shaped building in the centre of the grand mosque in Makkah.

Madinah A city where the Prophet Muhammad ﷺ lived, and where he is buried.

Makkah The city where the Prophet Muhammad ﷺ was born.

mosque A building where Muslims meet and worship.

Muslims People who believe in Islam.

Qur'an The name given to the Muslim Holy Book.

Prophet A person chosen by Allah to instruct people as to the will of Allah. Muhammad ﷺ was chosen as a prophet.

Ramadan The ninth month of the Muslim calendar. During Ramadan Muslims do not eat or drink between sunrise and sunset.

30

Further Information

Books to Read

A Year of Religious Festivals:
My Muslim Year by Cath Senker
(Hodder Wayland, 2004)

Celebrations!: Ramadan and Id-ul-Fitr by
Mandy Ross (Heinemann, 2002)

Hajj Stories by Anita Ganeri
(Evans Brothers, 2004)

Holy Places: Makkah by Mandy Ross
(Heinemann, 2003)

Our Culture: Muslim by Jenny Wood
(Franklin Watts, 2003)

Places of Worship: Mosques
(Heinemann, 1999)

Talking About My Faith: I am Muslim
by Cath Senker (Franklin Watts, 2005)

The Facts About Islam by Alison Cooper
(Hodder Wayland, 2006)

Useful Organisations

The Islamic Foundation
Markfield Conference Centre,
Ratby Lane,
Markfield,
Leicestershire
LE67 9SY
Tel: 01530 244944
www.islamic-foundation.org.uk

Muslim Educational Trust
130 Stroud Green Road,
London
N4 3RZ
Tel: 020 7272 8502
www.muslim-ed-trust.org.uk

IQRA Trust
3rd Floor
16 Grosvenor Crescent,
London
SW1X 7EP
Tel: 020 7838 7987
www.iqratrust.org

The website addresses (URLs) included in
this book were valid at the time of going to
press. However, because of the nature of the
Internet, it is possible that some addresses
may have changed, or sites may have
changed or closed down since publication.
While the authors and Publisher regret any
inconvenience this may cause readers, no
responsibility for any such changes can be
accepted by either the authors or the
Publisher.

Index